HOW TO BECOME
A VIRTUAL ASSISTANT

Table of Contents

HOW TO BECOME A VIRTUAL ASSISTANT

Preface

Who runs the world? Virtual assistants! In this book, you'll learn how to become the ultimate girl boss by harnessing the power of your virtual assistant skills. With tips on finding and attracting clients, managing your business, and expanding your services, you'll be able to conquer the virtual world and achieve your dreams. So grab your laptop, your favorite power suit, and get ready to rule the virtual assistant game like the girl boss you were born to be.

Welcome to the virtual world, where the coffee is always hot and the commute is nonexistent. In this brave new digital age, the role of the virtual assistant has become increasingly important.

From scheduling appointments to managing emails, virtual assistants are the unsung heroes of the online world. But what does it take to become a virtual assistant? Is it all about typing speed and good grammar? Or do you need to be a master of all trades, from social media management to project coordination?

In this ebook, we'll explore the ins and outs of becoming a virtual assistant. We'll dive into the skills and tools you need to succeed in this dynamic and ever-evolving field. We'll also tackle some of the common misconceptions about virtual assistants, such as the idea that they're just glorified data entry clerks.

So, whether you're a seasoned admin looking to make the switch to virtual or a tech-savvy newbie eager to learn the ropes, this ebook is your go-to guide for becoming a top-notch virtual assistant. Get ready to ditch the cubicle and embrace the digital lifestyle. The virtual world is waiting for you!

So grab a cup of coffee, put on your sassiest outfit, and get ready to rock your virtual assistant business like the sexy boss you are.

Introduction

Are you tired of the daily grind of commuting to an office, sitting in a cubicle, and enduring awkward water cooler conversations? Do you dream of a career that o ers flexibility, freedom, and an endless supply of coffee? Well, my friend, it's time to enter the wonderful world of virtual assisting.

As a virtual assistant, you'll have the power to work from anywhere in the world, wearing your pajamas and sipping a latte (or a martini, no judgment here). You'll be the ultimate multitasker, juggling multiple clients and projects with ease. You'll be the master of your own schedule, taking on as much or as little work as you like. And best of all, you'll be part of a growing industry that's changing the way we work and live.

But don't be fooled by the allure of the virtual life. Being a virtual assistant takes hard work, dedication, and a willingness to learn new skills. That's why we've created this ebook, to guide you on your journey to becoming a virtual assistant extraordinaire.

In these pages, we'll cover everything from the basics of virtual assisting to advanced skills like project management and social media marketing. We'll share tips and tricks from seasoned virtual assistants who've been there, done that, and are still rocking their virtual businesses. And we'll debunk some of the myths and misconceptions about virtual assisting that might be holding you back.

So, whether you're a seasoned pro looking to up your game or a newbie just dipping your toes into the virtual waters, this ebook is for you. Get ready to say goodbye to the 9-to-5 and hello to a career that's as flexible, fun, and fulfilling as you are. Let's get started!

Chapter One
The Ultimate Guide
to Becoming a Virtual Assistant
(and Actually Liking Your Job)

Welcome to the wonderful world of virtual assistance! If you've ever dreamed of working from home, setting your own hours, and having the freedom to choose your clients and projects, then becoming a virtual assistant might just be the perfect career choice for you.

But first, what is a virtual assistant, you ask? Well, simply put, a virtual assistant (or VA for short) is a self-employed professional who provides administrative, technical, or creative assistance to clients remotely, using technology such as email, instant messaging, and video conferencing. In other words, you get to be your own boss and work from the comfort of your own home, while helping other businesses and individuals run their operations smoothly.

So why become a virtual assistant? Well, the benefits are numerous. For starters, you get to choose your own clients and projects, so you can specialize in the areas that interest you the most. Plus, you get to work from anywhere in the world, as long as you have an internet connection. No more commuting or dealing with o ce politics! And let's not forget the flexibility of being able to set your own schedule and work as much or as little as you want.

In this ebook, we'll cover everything you need to know to become a successful virtual assistant, from finding your niche and building your brand, to setting your rates and finding clients. We'll also provide you with tips and tricks on how to stay organized, motivated, and productive, even when working from home. So buckle up and get ready to take your first step towards a fulfilling and rewarding career as a virtual assistant!

Chapter 2

Who Needs Superpowers
When You've Got Skills and Passions?

Welcome back, my dear reader! If you're still with me, then congratulations, you've made it to Chapter 2. Now, let's get down to business and start assessing your skills and interests. But don't worry, it won't be as painful as a visit to the dentist.

First things first, let's identify your strengths and weaknesses. Remember, we're not here to judge you, just to help you become the best virtual assistant you can be. So, take a deep breath and ask yourself, "What am I good at?" and "What could I improve on?" Be honest with yourself, but don't be too hard on yourself either. We all have areas we excel in and areas we struggle with.

Next, let's determine your interests and passions. What gets you excited and motivated? What could you talk about for hours without getting bored? It's important to find a job that aligns with your interests and passions because it will make your work more fulfilling and enjoyable. Plus, if you're passionate about something, you'll naturally be better at it.

Now, let's talk about the skills needed to become a virtual assistant. Don't worry, you don't need to be a superhero with a cape and a catchy theme song. But you do need some skills to succeed in this line of work. Here are some of the most important ones:

- Communication: As a virtual assistant, you'll be communicating with clients on a regular basis. You need to be able to articulate yourself clearly and e ectively through email, phone, and video calls.

- Organization: You'll be juggling multiple tasks and clients at once, so you need to be organized and able to prioritize your workload.

- Time management: Speaking of workload, you need to be able to manage your time e ectively to meet deadlines and deliver quality work.

- Tech-savviness: As a virtual assistant, you'll be working with various software and tools. You need to be comfortable with technology and able to learn new programs quickly.

- Problem-solving: You'll encounter challenges along the way, so you need to be able to think on your feet and come up with creative solutions.

There you have it, folks! Assessing your skills and interests, identifying your strengths and weaknesses, determining your passions, and understanding the necessary skills to be a virtual assistant. Don't worry if you don't tick all the boxes right now. With practice and dedication, you can acquire and hone these skills. And who knows, you might even discover a few superpowers along the way!

Chapter 3

The Business Name Game and Other Adventures in Starting Your Own Virtual Assistant Business

Welcome to Chapter 3, where we'll be diving into the exciting world of setting up your own virtual assistant business. Grab a pen, a notepad, and maybe a drink, because things are about to get serious (and by serious, I mean fun and exhilarating).

First things first, let's choose a business name. This is where you get to let your creativity shine. Do you want a name that's witty, catchy, or simple and straightforward? The choice is yours, but make sure it's something that reflects your brand and is memorable for your clients. And hey, if you're really struggling to come up with a name, just pick a random object from your desk and add "VA" to the end of it. Voila, you're now "StaplerVA" or "MousepadVA". Okay, maybe don't do that, but you get the idea.

Choosing a business name for your virtual assistant business is like picking a password - it needs to be both memorable and secure. So, avoid cliches like "Virtual Virtuoso" or "Admin Ace" unless you want to be mistaken for a magician. If you're stuck for ideas, don't worry! There are plenty of online resources to help you brainstorm. You could try a business name generator or even consult with a professional namer. Just make sure to avoid any names that are already trademarked or too similar to existing businesses. After all, you don't want to end up in a legal battle with a virtual rival over a name like "Virtual Vixen."

Stand Out

Let's talk about how to make yourself stand out from the sea of other VAs out there. It's time to build a brand that's as edgy and memorable as you are. Here are some tips on how to brand yourself as a virtual assistant:

- Discover your niche: What makes you unique? Do you specialize in email marketing, graphic design, or maybe something even more niche? Whatever it is, make sure you identify your niche so you can target the right clients.

- Develop a badass brand identity: This means creating a logo, picking a color scheme, and coming up with a kickass tagline. Make sure your brand identity is consistent across all your marketing materials so people will recognize you.

- Create a killer website: Your website is the first impression potential clients will have of you, so make sure it's on point. Make it professional and easy to navigate, and don't forget to include testimonials from happy clients.

- Get social: Social media is your friend, people! Find out where your ideal clients are hanging out and make sure you're there too. Share valuable content, engage with others, and promote your services.

- Network like a boss: Building relationships is key to success in any industry. Attend virtual conferences, join online networking groups, and collaborate on projects to build your network and expand your reach.

Remember, branding is all about telling a story that connects with your audience. By discovering your niche, developing a killer brand identity, creating a killer website, getting social, and networking like a boss, you can create a memorable brand that stands out from the crowd. Let's do this, VAs!

Structure

Now, the burning question on your mind might be: should you structure your business as a sole proprietorship or an LLC? This might sound boring, but it's important to understand the legal implications of each option. And let me tell you, my dear friend, that's a decision not to be taken lightly.

First of all, let's talk about sole proprietorships. They're like the wild west of the business world, where you're the sheri , the outlaw, and the whole darn town all rolled into one. As a sole proprietor, you're the sole owner of your business and responsible for all its debts and obligations. Sure, it might sound lonely, but hey, you're the boss!

On the other hand, we have LLCs, or Limited Liability Companies. Think of them as the fancy, high-class establishment that only admits members with a secret handshake. As an LLC, your personal assets are protected from business debts and obligations, and you get to enjoy the perks of limited liability.

So, which one should you choose? It really depends on your personal preferences and the level of risk you're willing to take. If you're a lone wolf who wants full control over their business, and you're not too worried about potential lawsuits or debts, then a sole proprietorship might be the way to go.

However, if you're looking for a bit more protection and want to separate your personal assets from your business, then an LLC is definitely worth considering. Plus, with an LLC, you'll have the added benefit of credibility and professionalism that comes with being a member of an established business entity.

At the end of the day, whether you choose a sole proprietorship or an LLC, what really matters is that you're passionate about your business and willing to put in the work to make it successful. Do your research, and consult with a lawyer or accountant if necessary. So go ahead, make your choice, and let the adventure begin!

Business Plan

So, now you've got a great virtual assistant business in the works and you're ready to take the world by storm. That's fantastic! But before you start counting your millions, you need to create a business plan.

I know, I know, you're thinking "but I just want to get started already!" But trust me, a business plan will save you time and headaches in the long run. It doesn't have to be a 100-page document, just a clear outline of your goals, target market, services, pricing, and marketing strategies. Plus, it will impress potential clients and investors, making you look like a pro.

Don't worry, it's not as daunting as it sounds. Here's how to do it in the most simple way possible:

- Start with the basics. Who are you? What do you want to sell? Who do you want to sell it to? Write down the answers to these questions, and you've already got the start of your business plan.

- Get to know your competition. Do some research on other VAs in your industry. What are they doing well? What could they improve on? Use this information to create a strategy that sets you apart from the rest.

- Crunch some numbers. How much money do you need to get started? How much will you charge for your product or service? How many sales do you need to break even? These are all important questions to answer, so make sure you're thorough.

- Create a marketing plan. How will you get the word out about your business? Which online platforms will you advertise on? Will you attend trade shows or conferences? Outline a plan that works for you and your budget.

● Review and revise. Once you've got a draft of your business plan, review it and make any necessary changes. Get feedback from friends, family, or other entrepreneurs to make sure you're on the right track.

See? Creating a business plan doesn't have to be scary. Just take it one step at a time, and you'll be on your way to entrepreneurial success in no time.

Online Presence

Last but not least, let's set up a website and social media presence. This is where you can showcase your skills, experience, and personality to potential clients. You don't need to be a web design wizard or a social media influencer, just make sure your website is user-friendly and your social media posts are engaging and relevant. And hey, if you're not comfortable with technology, just hire someone to do it for you. That's the beauty of being a virtual assistant, you have access to a global pool of talented professionals.

So, there you have it! Choosing a business name, deciding on a legal structure, creating a business plan, and setting up a website and social media presence. Don't let these steps intimidate you, they're all part of the adventure of starting your own business. And who knows, maybe you'll end up becoming the next big thing in the virtual assistant world. Now go forth and conquer!

Chapter 4

Hunting for Clients: A Virtual Assistant's Guide to Finding and Attracting Business

Welcome to Chapter 4, where we'll be discussing the art of finding and attracting clients. This is where things get exciting, my friends, because it's time to put your skills to the test and show the world what you're made of.

Targeting

First things first, let's identify your target market. Trying to sell your virtual assistant services to everyone is like trying to sell a vegan burger to a meat lover - it's not going to work!

Who says there's a one-size-fits-all target market for a virtual assistant business? Start by asking yourself, who needs your services the most? Who are you trying to reach? Are you a whiz at admin tasks? Then small business owners may be your perfect match. Small business owners may need help with administrative tasks, or busy executives who need someone to manage their calendars and emails. Or maybe you're a social media maven - in that case, entrepreneurs could be your jam. Busy executives drowning in emails? You could be their lifesaver! Maybe you're after solopreneurs looking for a helping hand with growing their online presence. They're out there too! Make yourself the go-to virtual assistant for your chosen target market.

Once you've identified your target market, you can focus your marketing efforts and create a customized approach that speaks directly to their needs. Trust me, it's easier to hit the bullseye when you're aiming at a specific target!

Marketing

Next up, let's talk marketing strategies. Don't worry, you don't need a fancy marketing degree or a huge budget to attract clients. Here are some effective (and budget-friendly) marketing strategies:

- Networking: Attend virtual events, join online communities, and reach out to people in your industry. Build relationships and over value, and you'll soon find yourself with a network of potential clients.

- Social media: Use social media platforms to showcase your skills, share valuable content, and engage with your audience. Make sure your profiles are professional and reflect your brand.

- Referrals: Word of mouth is a powerful tool, so don't be afraid to ask your satisfied clients for referrals. Offer a discount or other incentives to encourage them to spread the word.

- Cold emailing: Reach out to potential clients via email and offer them a free consultation or sample of your work. Make sure your emails are personalized and show how your services can benefit their business.

Portfolio

Alright my fellow virtual assistant superheroes, it's time to talk about one of the most important aspects of attracting new clients – creating a killer portfolio. Think of it as your virtual assistant bat signal – it's your way of showcasing your skills and abilities to the world.

This is where you get to shine and show potential clients what you're capable of. Include examples of your work, testimonials from satisfied clients, and a clear description of your services and pricing. Make sure your portfolio is visually appealing and easy to navigate.

So how do you create a portfolio that will make potential clients weak in the knees? Here are some tips:

❖ Show, don't tell – Don't just tell potential clients that you're a rockstar VA, show them! Include examples of your work that demonstrate your skills and expertise. Whether it's social media management, graphic design, or copywriting, make sure you're showcasing your best work.

❖ Get testimonials – There's nothing more persuasive than glowing testimonials from satisfied clients. Reach out to past clients and ask them to share their experience working with you. Trust me, potential clients will eat it up.

❖ Be clear about your services and pricing – No one likes a mystery, especially when it comes to pricing. Be upfront about what services you offer and how much they cost. This will save you time and headaches down the line.

❖ Make it visually appealing – Your portfolio should be visually appealing and easy to navigate. Use high-quality images and make sure the layout is easy to follow. Bonus points if you add some personality to your portfolio – after all, you're not just a robot churning out work, you're a badass virtual assistant!

Take these tips on creating a killer portfolio and make potential clients drool with anticipation. Go showcase those skills!

So, there you have it, my lovelies! Identifying your target market, using effective marketing strategies, and creating a portfolio that showcases your skills. Don't be afraid to put yourself out there and take risks. Remember, the more you put yourself in front of potential clients, the more likely they are to hire you. Now go hunt for those clients!

Chapter 5

Juggling Act: How to Manage Your Virtual Assistant Business Like a Pro

Welcome to Chapter 5, where we'll be discussing the art of managing your virtual assistant business. This is where things get real, my friends, because it's time to put on your business hat and get down to the nitty-gritty of running a successful operation.

First things first, let's talk time management. As a virtual assistant, your time is your most valuable asset, so it's important to use it wisely. Here are some time management tips to help you stay on track:

- Set priorities: Make a list of your tasks for the day and prioritize them based on their importance and deadline.

- Use a calendar: Use a calendar or scheduling tool to manage your time and stay organized.

- Take breaks: Take breaks throughout the day to avoid burnout and keep your energy levels up.

- Say no: Don't be afraid to say no to tasks that don't align with your skills or values.

Alrighty, buckle up and hold on tight because I'm about to spill the beans on the best apps and tools to use in your virtual assistant business. And let me tell you, my friend, these are not your grandma's tools.

First up, we have Trello. This bad boy is like a virtual bulletin board on steroids. With Trello, you can organize your to-do list, keep track of deadlines, and collaborate with your clients in real-time. Plus, it's got a slick interface that'll make you feel like a boss.

Next, we have Calendly. Say goodbye to the back-and-forth of scheduling appointments with clients. Calendly lets you send out your availability and lets clients book a time that works for them. It's like having a personal assistant without having to pay someone else's salary.

Now, let's talk about Zoom. This app needs no introduction, but I'll give you one anyway. Zoom is the ultimate virtual meeting tool that lets you connect with clients from anywhere in the world. Plus, it's got nifty features like screen sharing and virtual backgrounds that'll make you look like a pro.

Last but not least, we have Slack. Think of Slack as your virtual water cooler. It's a messaging app that lets you communicate with clients and team members in real-time. Plus, it's got some neat integrations with other apps, so you can streamline your workflow and get more done in less time.

So there you have it, some of the best tools to use in your never-ending quest for productivity and world domination! That's not to say there aren't a ton more out there that you might like to work with. By all means, try different apps to see what you like. With these invaluable resources at your fingertips, you'll be unstoppable, darling. They will help you stay organized, focused, and on top of your game. So go forth, my sweetie darlings, and conquer the world with the power of technology!

Rates and Invoicing

Ah, invoicing and rates – the bane of every virtual assistant's existence. It can be daunting to figure out how much to charge for your services, but don't sell yourself short. Fear not, my fellow hustlers, for I have some tips to help you navigate this murky territory with style.

First things first, let's talk rates. You might be tempted to lowball yourself, thinking that you'll attract more clients that way. But let me tell you, that's a rookie mistake. You need to value your time and expertise and charge accordingly. Do your research, see what other virtual assistants in your niche are charging, and then add a little extra for your badassery. After all, you're not just an assistant – you're a ninja, a magician, a superhero in disguise.

Now, onto invoicing. This can be a tricky business, especially if you're dealing with clients who are slow to pay or just plain flaky. My advice? Be firm but fair. Set clear payment terms upfront, and make sure your clients understand that you mean business. Send out your invoices on time, and don't be afraid to follow up if payment is overdue. And if all else fails, unleash your inner badass and start sending out strongly worded emails – trust me, it works like a charm.

In the end, invoicing and rates might seem like boring administrative tasks, but they're crucial to the success of your virtual assistant business. It can be daunting to figure out how much to charge for your services, but don't sell yourself short. Do your research and make sure your rates are competitive and reflect your skills and experience. When it comes to invoicing, make sure you have a clear system in place and send invoices promptly to avoid any confusion or delays. So don't be afraid to demand what you're worth – after all, you're a virtual assistant, not a doormat.

Building relationships with clients

This is where you get to flex your people skills and show your clients that you're not just a robot behind a computer screen. Here are some tips for building strong relationships with your clients:

- Communicate regularly: Keep your clients updated on your progress and don't be afraid to ask for feedback.

- Be reliable: Stick to deadlines and make sure your clients can rely on you to deliver high-quality work.

- Be proactive: Anticipate your clients' needs and offer solutions before they even ask.

● Show your personality: Let your clients get to know you and your personality. Building a connection can help build trust and lead to long-term relationships.

You're doing fabulous, darling! Time management tips, setting rates and invoicing, and building relationships with clients. Remember, managing your virtual assistant business is all about finding balance and staying organized.

Now, keep shining and manage like a boss!

Chapter 6
Diversify or Die:

How to Expand Your Virtual Assistant Services Like a Pro

Welcome to Chapter 6, where we'll be discussing the art of expanding your virtual assistant services. This is where things get exciting, my friends, because it's time to explore new avenues and take your business to the next level.

Alright, my fellow virtual assistant hustlers, it's time to get our thinking caps on and brainstorm some new services to offer! Now, I know what you're thinking – "But I'm just a virtual assistant, I can't possibly offer anything else!" – but trust me, the world is your oyster.

Finding Your Niche

First things first, let's talk about identifying new services to offer. As a virtual assistant, you're not limited to just one skillset. Take a look at your strengths and interests and think outside the box. Could you offer social media management? Graphic design? Copywriting? The possibilities are endless, so don't be afraid to get creative.

Take a good hard look at your strengths and interests. Are you a whiz at social media? Do you have an eye for design? Are you a wordsmith extraordinaire? Whatever your talents may be, there's a way to monetize them and offer them as a service.

But don't just limit yourself to the obvious choices – think outside the box, my friends! Maybe you're a master of organization and could o er virtual decluttering services. Or perhaps you're a fitness fanatic and could offer virtual workout coaching. The possibilities are endless, and the only limit is your imagination.

So let's get creative, my darlings! It's time to unleash our inner entrepreneurial spirits and offer some killer new services. Who knows, you might just stumble upon your new niche and become the go-to virtual assistant for that particular skillset.

Never Stop Learning!

Let's talk about developing new skills. It's important to stay up-to-date with the latest trends and technologies in your industry. Take courses, attend workshops, and read industry blogs to stay on top of your game. This will not only help you o er new services but also improve the quality of your existing work.

Grow, Baby!

Now, let's chat about growing your business. This is where you get to flex your entrepreneurial muscles and take your business to the next level. Here are some tips for growing your virtual assistant business:

→ Hire help: If you're overwhelmed with work, consider hiring other virtual assistants to help you out.

Alright, my fellow virtual assistant bosses, let's talk about outsourcing – because let's face it, sometimes we just can't do it all ourselves. When your virtual assistant business is booming and your to-do list is a mile long, it's time to call in the cavalry and outsource some tasks.

First things first, let's talk about finding the right people for the job. Don't just settle for the first person who pops up on Fiverr – do your research and find someone who's a good fit for your business and has the skills to match. And remember, just because you're outsourcing doesn't mean you're off the hook – you still need to manage the project and make sure everything's on track.

But once you've found your dream team, it's time to sit back, relax, and let them work their magic. Whether it's data entry, research, or social media management, outsourcing can free up your time and energy so you can focus on the big picture – growing your business and slaying the competition.

Of course, outsourcing isn't a one-size-fits-all solution, and it's not for everyone. But if you find yourself drowning in a sea of virtual assistant tasks and can't keep your head above water, it might be time to consider outsourcing. And who knows – you might just discover a new passion for managing a team and become the ultimate virtual assistant boss.

→ Raise your rates: As your skills and experience grow, don't be afraid to raise your rates to reflect your value.

Ah, the age-old question – when is it time to raise your rates as a virtual assistant? Well, my dear hustlers, the answer is simple: when you're so in-demand that you're turning away clients left and right.

You see, sweetie, when you're just starting out as a virtual assistant, it's important to price yourself competitively to attract clients. But as you gain experience, build your skills, and become a sought-after VA superstar, it's time to bump up those rates and start charging what you're worth.

So how do you know when the time is right? Well, if you find yourself with a waitlist of clients begging to work with you, it's a pretty good sign that you're ready for a rate increase. And don't be afraid to be upfront with your clients about it – they'll understand that your time is valuable and that you're worth the investment.

But remember, my darlings, with great rates comes great responsibility. You need to make sure you're delivering top-notch work and providing exceptional value to your clients. And if you ever start feeling overwhelmed or overworked, it might be time to reassess your workload and adjust your rates accordingly.

In the end, raising your rates as a virtual assistant is all about knowing your worth, providing excellent service, and staying on top of your game. So go forth and slay, my virtual assistant queens and kings – you're worth every penny!

→ Expand your network: Attend industry events and join online communities to expand your network and attract new clients.

Alright my fellow virtual assistant rockstars, let's talk about expanding our networks and attracting new clients – because let's face it, we can never have too many clients, am I right?

One of the best ways to do this is by joining online communities where we can connect with other like-minded individuals and showcase our skills. There are a ton of great communities out there, so let's dive in and check out some of the best ones:

★ Facebook Groups – Yes, I know, Facebook can be a black hole of memes and cat videos, but it's also a treasure trove of virtual assistant groups where you can network with other VAs, share tips and tricks, and even find new clients.

★ LinkedIn Groups – If you're more of a professional type, LinkedIn Groups are a great place to connect with other professionals in your industry and show off your expertise.

★ Reddit – Don't underestimate the power of Reddit – there are a ton of great subreddits dedicated to entrepreneurship, freelancing, and virtual assisting, where you can connect with other VAs and get valuable advice.

★ Slack Communities – Slack is a popular communication platform for remote teams, and there are plenty of Slack communities for virtual assistants where you can connect with others and even find new clients.

★ Online Forums – Last but not least, there are a ton of online forums dedicated to virtual assisting and freelancing, where you can connect with others, share your experiences, and learn from the pros.

So there you have it, my virtual assistant comrades – some of the best online communities to expand your network and attract new clients. Don't be afraid to jump in, make connections, and show off your skills –because you never know who might be looking for a virtual assistant just like you!

→ Create passive income streams: Consider creating digital products or courses to generate passive income and grow your business.

Oh, passive income – it's the dream of every virtual assistant, isn't it? I mean, who doesn't want to make money while they sleep, am I right? Well, fear not my dear virtual assistants, because I'm here to spill the tea on how you can create passive income streams as a VA.

First things first, you need to think outside the box. Yes, you can offer your services as a VA, but what else can you do? Here are some ideas to get those creative juices flowing:

★ Create digital products – As a VA, you have a ton of skills that others might be willing to pay for. So why not create digital products like templates, courses, or e-books that you can sell on your website or platforms like Etsy?

★ Affiliate marketing – You can also make some extra cash by promoting other people's products or services through affiliate marketing. If you have a blog or social media following, this can be a great way to earn some passive income.

★ Sell your photos or videos – If you have a knack for photography or videography, you can sell your content on platforms like Shutterstock or iStock and earn royalties every time someone downloads it.

★ Offer ad space – Do you have a popular blog or website? Consider offering ad space to others and earn passive income every time someone clicks on an ad.

So there you have it, my fellow hustlers – some ideas for creating passive income streams as a virtual assistant. Just remember, the key is to think outside the box and find ways to leverage your skills and expertise. Now go forth and make that money while you sleep!

You're crushing it, my lovelies! Identifying new services to offer, developing new skills, and growing your business. Remember, the sky's the limit when it comes to your virtual assistant business. Stay curious, stay innovative, and always be willing to take risks. Bravo, darling! You're doing amazing and diversifying like a boss!

Chapter 7

From VA to VIP: The Best Resources and Mentors for Virtual Assistants!

Looking for some resources to help you step up your game? Well, you've come to the right place! Here are some places you can find all the tools, tips, and tricks you need to become the best virtual assistant you can be:

- Online Forums: Virtual assistants often congregate in online forums, sharing knowledge and resources. Check out sites like Reddit or Facebook groups to find communities of like-minded individuals who can help you hone your skills.

- YouTube tutorials: If you're a visual learner, you'll love the vast array of tutorials available on YouTube. Whether you need to learn how to use a new software program or master a new skill, there's sure to be a tutorial out there for you.

- Blogs: Virtual assistants who blog often share their knowledge and experience, so it's worth checking out some VA blogs to see what's out there. Some popular ones include The Virtual Savvy, Horkey Handbook, and Gina Horkey.

- Webinars and online courses: Many virtual assistants offer webinars or online courses on a variety of topics. Whether you want to learn how to market yourself better, improve your writing skills, or manage your time more efficiently, there's a course out there for you.

Now, if you're looking for a mentor, there are a few places you can turn to:

- LinkedIn: This is a great place to find professionals in your field who can offer guidance and support. Don't be afraid to reach out and ask for advice!

- Industry associations: There are a number of industry associations that cater specifically to virtual assistants, such as the International Virtual Assistants Association. These associations often offer mentorship programs or can put you in touch with more experienced virtual assistants.
- Local networking groups: Look for local networking groups in your area where you can meet other virtual assistants and potentially find a mentor.

Remember, becoming a successful virtual assistant takes time and effort, but with the right resources and mentorship, you can achieve your goals and grow your business.

Conclusion: You're a Virtual Superstar!

Congratulations, my dear reader, you've made it to the end of this book! By now, you should be feeling pretty confident in your ability to become a virtual assistant and take the world by storm.

Let's take a moment to recap the benefits of becoming a virtual assistant:

- Freedom: You get to work from anywhere in the world, on your own terms.

- Flexibility: You get to set your own schedule and work as much or as little as you want.

- Variety: You get to work with a variety of clients and industries, keeping your work fresh and exciting.

- Creativity: You get to use your creativity and problem-solving skills to help your clients succeed.

- Income potential: You get to earn a great income doing work that you love.

Now, I know that starting a new career can be daunting, but I want to encourage you to pursue your goals. Remember, every successful person started somewhere, and with the right mindset and determination, you can achieve anything you set your mind to.

Before I sign off, I want to leave you with some final thoughts and resources for further reading. Always be open to learning and growing, both professionally and personally. Keep up with industry trends, and don't be afraid to experiment with new services and approaches.

And if you ever need a little inspiration or guidance, don't hesitate to check out some of the many resources available online, from industry blogs to online communities to courses and workshops.

So, my dear reader, go forth and become the virtual superstar I know you can be!